westermann

W0083858

Textbook 4

Herausgegeben von
Gisela Ehlers

Erarbeitet von
Gisela Ehlers, Anna Van Montagu,
Matthias Muth, Michaela Schönau,
Hannelore Tait

Auf der Grundlage der Ausgaben
Bumblebee 3/4 (2013/2014) und
Bumblebee 1-4 (2014-2016)
von Gisela Ehlers, Grit Kahstein, Christina Meindl,
Ursula Michailow-Drews, Anna Van Montagu,
Matthias Muth, Michaela Schönau, Hannelore Tait,
Anne Zeich-Pelsis

Illustriert von
Juliane Assies, Gabie Hilgert, Oda Ruthe,
Friederike Schumann sowie Iris Blanck,
Andrea Dölling, Elisabeth Holzhausen,
Markus Humbach

Contents

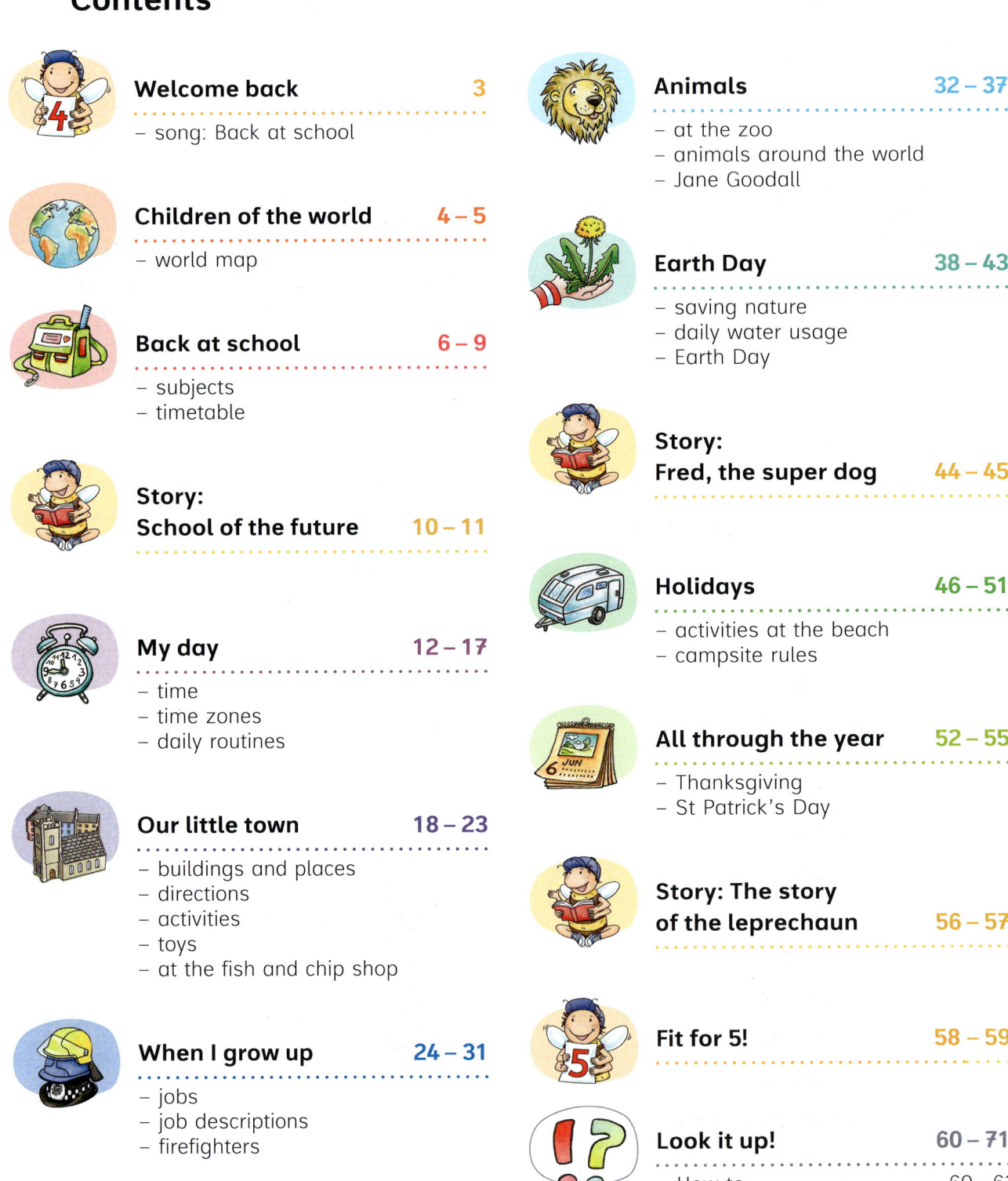

Welcome back

At school!

S-C-H-O-O-L! Back at school!

All my friends are back at school – school – back at school!
All my friends are back at school – school – back at school!

I can learn at school, I can learn at school
I can learn at school with all my friends!

 I can read …

 I can write …

 I can sing …

 I can speak …

 I can count …

 I can draw …

 I can play …

 I can dance …

1 👂 👄 Listen to the song. What is it about?

2 👂 📦 Listen again and read along.

3 👄 Join in.

Einen Rap verstehen und mitsprechen.
Wdh: activities
Diff ▼ Fö 1–2, **Diff** ▲ Fo 1–2

FC/WC 1–9
CD 1, 2 KV 1–4
WB S. 3

three / **3**

Children of the world

My name is Maureen.
I'm from Ireland.
My favourite colour is green.

Hi, I'm Matthew.
I live in Canada.
I like playing ice hockey.

Canada

Great Britain

Ireland

United States of America

I'm Samuel from the USA.
I live in New York.
I'm 10 years old.

I'm Gemma from South Africa.
My favourite pet is my dog.

1 👂👆 Listen and point.

2 👂📖 Listen again and read along.

3 👄 Talk about the children.

Matthew lives in Canada.
He likes playing ice hockey.

Selbstvorstellungen der Kinder verstehen. SuS können im Internet nach Informationen über die Länder suchen.
Diff ▼ Fö 3–5, Diff ▲ Fo 3–5

FC/WC 10–16
CD 3
WB S. 4/5

Hello, I'm John from England.
My favourite football team is Chelsea.

Hi, I'm Amy from Australia.
I've got 2 brothers and 2 sisters.

India

South Africa

Australia

New Zealand

Hello, I'm Raj from India.
My hobbies are swimming and reading.

My name is …
I live in …
I like …

4 👄 What about you? Give a short presentation.

Where do the children come from?
What language do the children speak?
Can you describe the flags?

KV 5–10

five / 5

Back at school

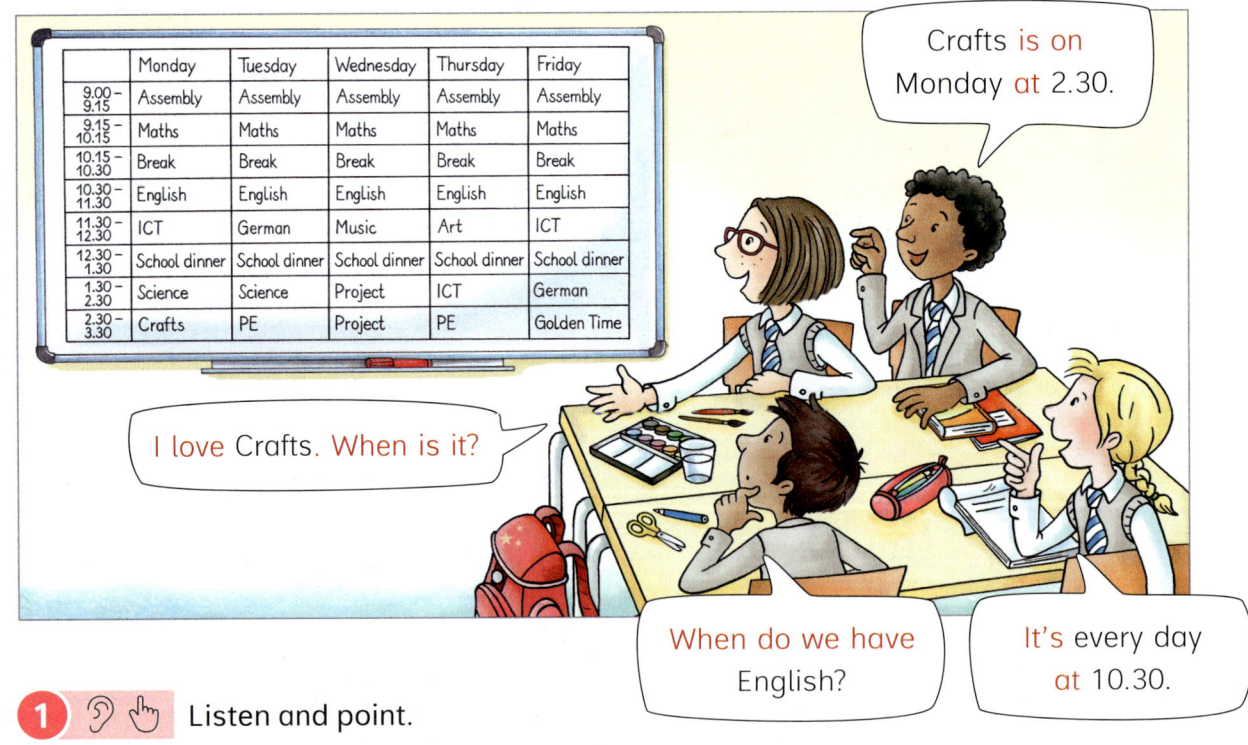

1 Listen and point.

2 Listen again and read along.

3 Do a role play.

Wdh: feelings
Diff ▼ Fö 6, **Diff** ▲ Fo 6
SuS können im Rollenspiel nach weiteren Fächern fragen.

CD 7

New words

1 👂👆 Listen and point.

2 👂📖 Listen and read along.

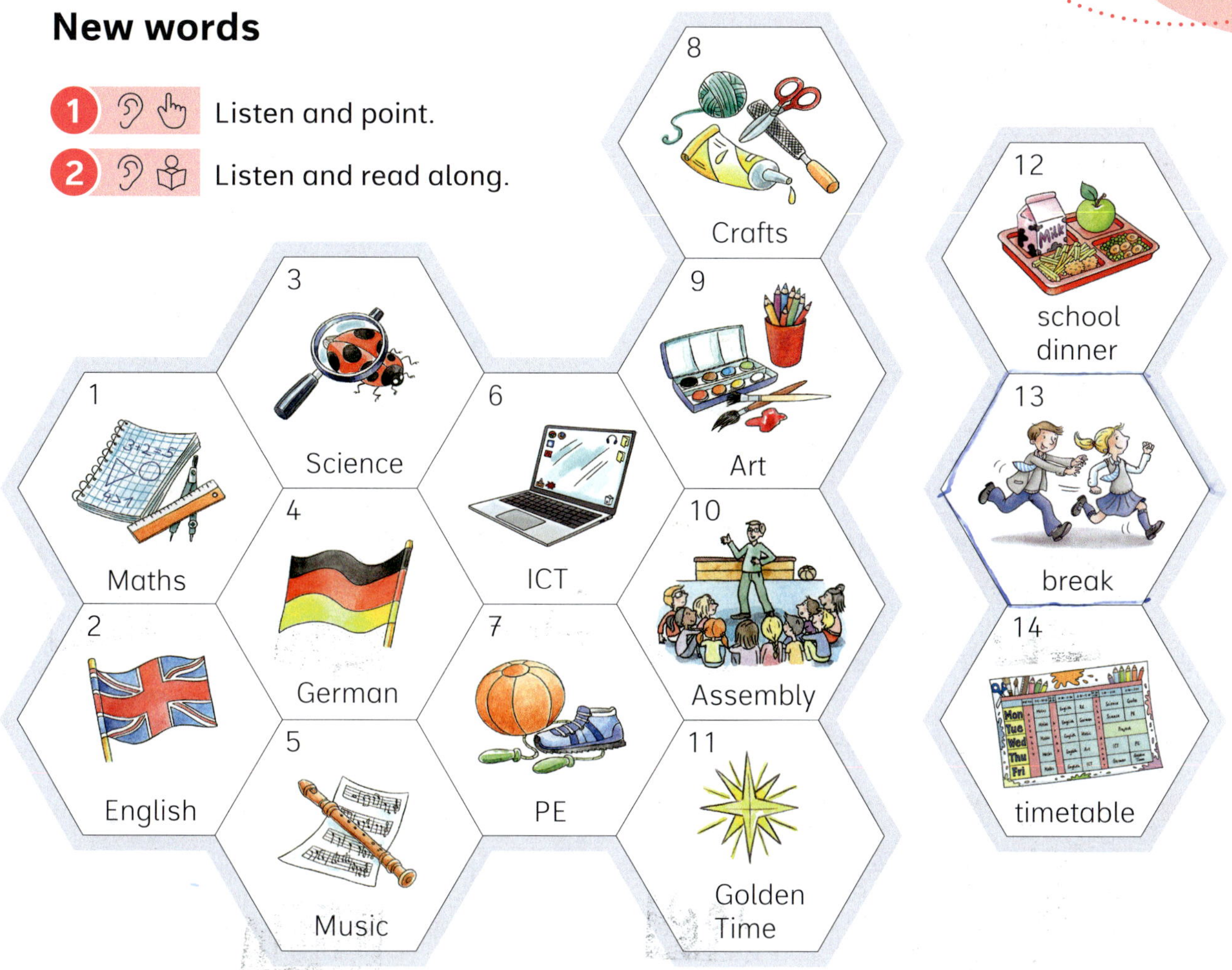

8 Crafts

3 Science

1 Maths

2 English

4 German

5 Music

6 ICT

7 PE

9 Art

10 Assembly

11 Golden Time

12 school dinner

13 break

14 timetable

3 📖 Read the dialogue.

4 👀👄 Practise the dialogue.

Do you like PE?

Yes, I do.

No, I don't!

What's your favourite subject?

My favourite subject is ICT.

Sich über Lieblingsschulfächer unterhalten.
Diff ▼ Fö 7, **Diff** ▲ Fo 7

FC/WC 17–30
CD 8
KV 11–15, 19

seven / **7**

Subjects

1 👂 📖 Listen and read along.

2 👄 Do the rap.

It's English now,
speak, speak, speak!

Now it's Art,
draw, draw, draw!

Then it's Maths,
count, count, count!

Music next,
sing, sing, sing!

It's German now,
read, read, read!

Golden Time,
fun, fun, fun!

3 📖 👄 Read Lisa's letter. Talk about it.

4 📱 Find more information about British schools.

Hi friends,

die Schule hat wieder angefangen und wir haben unseren neuen Stundenplan bekommen. Da gibt es zum Beispiel das Fach „ICT". Das steht für „Information and Communication Technology". Hier lernen wir, am Computer zu arbeiten. Das macht Spaß. Das Fach „Science" ist auch sehr interessant. Wir lernen eine Menge über Pflanzen und Tiere, machen Experimente und erfahren viel über die Geschichte Großbritanniens. Wenn wir „Golden Time" haben, können wir uns aussuchen, was wir am liebsten machen möchten. Ich hole mir dann gern Bücher aus unserer „library". In „PE", „Physical Education", spielen wir oft Mannschaftsspiele. In der Pause sind wir auf dem „school playground", dem Schulhof.

Love, Lisa

SuS sprechen über Aufbau, Funktion und Gestaltung des Briefes.

CD 9, 10
KV 17

LET'S TALK! **What I like about school**

1 👂📖 Listen and read along.

2 👀👄 Practise the dialogue.

3 ✏️ Write your own list: I like … / I don't like …

> I like Crafts but I don't like Maths.

> I like Music because I like singing.

> What subjects do you like?

> What subjects don't you like?

> I don't like Art because I don't like drawing.

			speaking.
I like …	Music	because I like …	drawing.
	Maths		reading.
	German		singing.
	English		learning about nature.
	PE		making things.
	Art		counting.
I don't like …	ICT	because I don't like …	working with computers.
	Science		playing ball games.
	Crafts		learning a language.

Diff ▼ Fö 8–9, Diff ▲ Fo 8–9
SuS formulieren weitere Begründungen.
L unterstützt dabei.

CD 11
KV 16, 18, 20
WB S. 9

nine / 9

School of the future

There is a new assistant teacher in class. It's Robo, a computer. All the children love him.

Robo is very clever. He likes Maths best because he likes counting.

Robo can do Maths fast. He is faster than all the children.

In the next PE lesson, they run races. Ben and Robo run first. They bump into each other.

Ben is okay but on Robo's head there are some red lights blinking.

The next day, something is wrong with Robo. He answers in German.

Eine Geschichte verstehen und nachspielen.
Diff ▼ L liest die Geschichte selbst.
Diff ▲ S gibt Inhalt der Geschichte auf Deutsch wieder.

Robo has problems with Maths.

Robo takes the watering can and waters some books. The children want to help him and take him to the ICT teacher.

The ICT teacher opens Robo. She finds the problem and repairs him.

Robo is fine again. He does all the Maths homework for the children because they helped him.

1 👂 🎁 Listen to the story and read along.

2 👄 What is the story about? Talk about it.

3 👓 Act out the story.

What can you see in the pictures?
Why does Robo speak German?
Would you like to have a robot in your class?

How to do a role play: S. 63
KV 21

eleven / 11

My day

09:00

At this moment,
it's 9 o'clock in London.
Lisa's school starts.

10:00

In Dresden, it's 10 o'clock now.
It's Anna's school break.

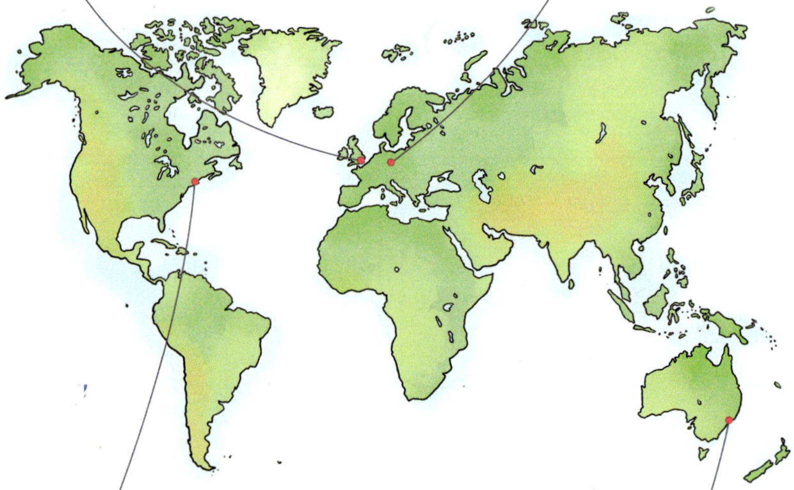

04:00

In New York City,
it's 4 o'clock in the morning.
Noah is asleep.

08:00

In Sydney, it's 8 o'clock
in the evening. Luke's favourite
TV programme is on.

1   Listen and point.

2   Talk about the children.

Über die Aktivitäten von Kindern in verschiedenen
Zeitzonen sprechen.

Daily activities

1 👂 ☝ Listen and point.

2 👂 📖 Listen and read along.

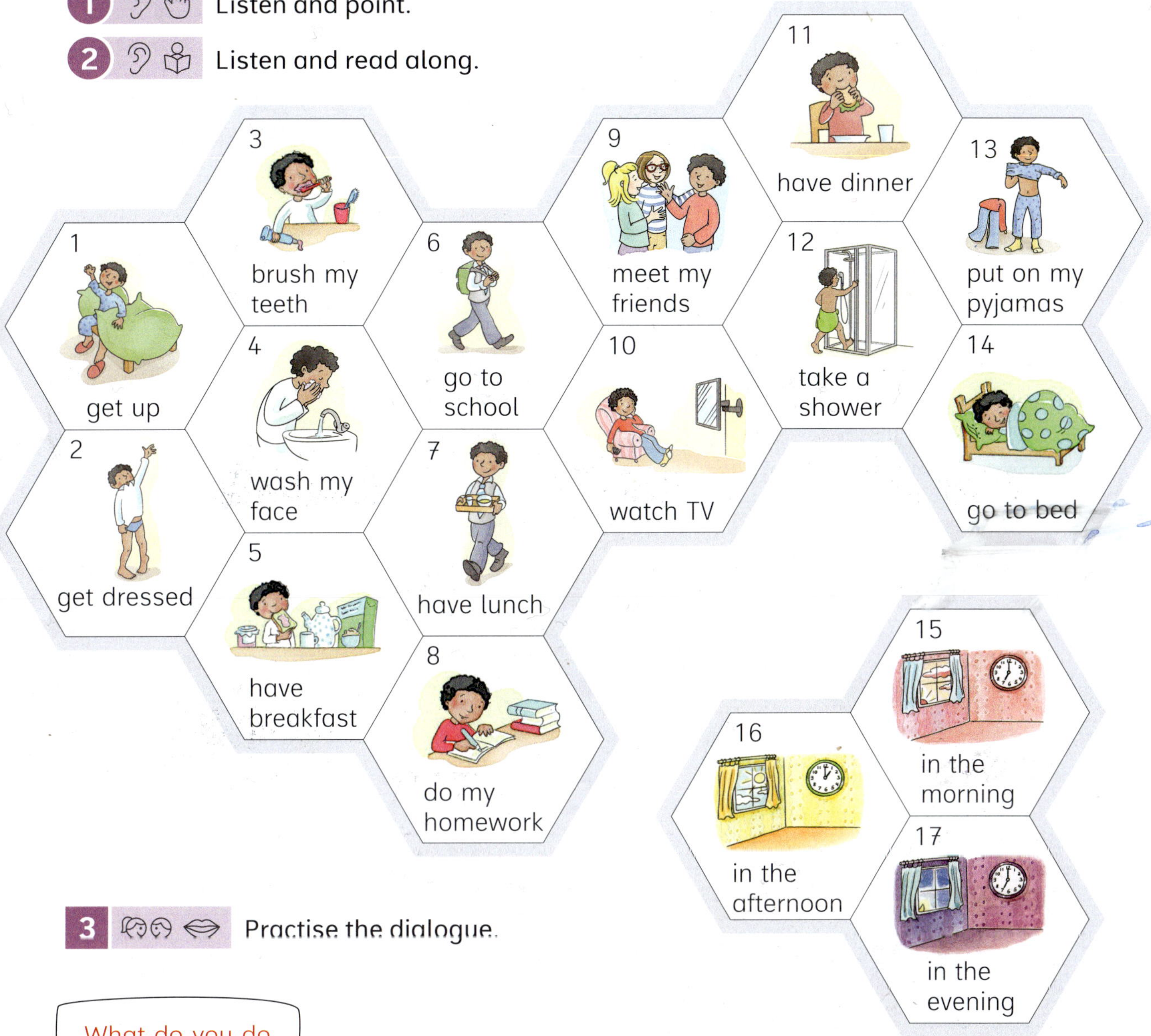

3 brush my teeth

1 get up

4 wash my face

2 get dressed

5 have breakfast

6 go to school

7 have lunch

8 do my homework

9 meet my friends

10 watch TV

11 have dinner

12 take a shower

13 put on my pyjamas

14 go to bed

15 in the morning

16 in the afternoon

17 in the evening

3 🗣🗣 👄 Practise the dialogue.

What do you do in the morning?

Every morning, I get up. I wash my face.

Sich über tägliche Gewohnheiten austauschen.
Diff ▾ Fö 11, **Diff** ▲ Fo 11

31–47
WB S. 11
23, 26, 29, 31

thirteen / **13**

LET'S TALK! **About my day**

1 👂👆 Listen and point.

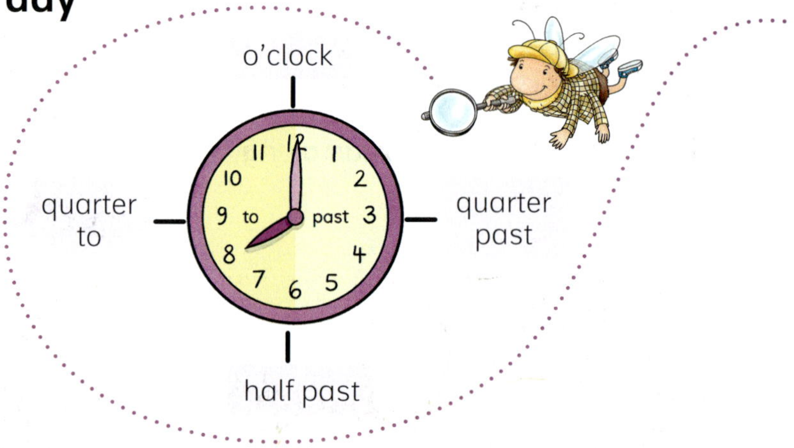

o'clock

quarter to

quarter past

half past

2 👀😊👄 Practise the dialogue.

When do you get up?

I get up at 7 o'clock.

When do you have dinner?

I have dinner at half past six.

Angaben zu Uhrzeiten und Aktivitäten machen.
Diff ▼ Fö 1... ...–14, **Diff** ▲ Fo 10, 12–14

FC/WC 48–51
CD 20 **KV** 24–25
WB S. 12

❯ Ich kann verstehen, wie Liam seinen Schultag verbringt.

Liam's day

1   Listen and point.

2   Listen and read along.

Hi, I'm Liam.
I live in Atlanta.
A typical school day
for me looks like this.

In the morning, I go to school by bus.

Our first lesson starts at 9 o'clock.

We have school dinner at 12 o'clock.

I often do my homework in the school library.

In the afternoon, I often play the guitar in the school band.

On Wednesday and Friday, I also play American football. It's my favourite school club.

Einer Foto-Geschichte landeskundliche Informationen entnehmen.

FC/WC 52–55
CD 23   KV 27, 30
WB S. 13

fifteen / 15

Time in Great Britain: a.m. and p.m.

1  Read Lisa's blog post. Talk about it.

http://lisa-in-great-britain.blog/

LISA IN GREAT BRITAIN

Hey ihr in Deutschland,

ihr glaubt nicht, was mir gestern passiert ist. Das war so peinlich.
Ben hatte mich zum Geburtstag eingeladen. In der Einladung stand
Come to my birthday party at 6:30 p.m.
Als ich bei Ben ankam, öffnete er erst nach dem zweiten Klingeln.
Er war erstaunt mich zu sehen. Als ich ihm erklärte, dass auf seiner
Einladung doch 6:30 stand, musste er plötzlich so lachen.
Er erklärte mir, dass bei englischen Uhrzeiten immer ein *a.m.* oder *p.m.*
nach den Ziffern stehen würde: *a.m.* bezeichnet die Stunden von Mitter-
nacht bis Mittag (also den Vormittag) und *p.m.* die Stunden von Mittag
bis Mitternacht (also den Nachmittag).
Ursprünglich kommen diese Bezeichnungen aus dem Lateinischen:
ante meridiem (a.m.) und *post meridiem (p.m.)*.
Ich bin dann nochmal nach Hause gefahren und abends
wieder hin. Die anderen haben ganz schön gelacht, als sie
von meinem Missgeschick erfahren haben.

Bis bald,
Lisa

Sich über Aufbau, Funktion und Gestaltung eines Blog-Eintrags
austauschen. Uhrzeitabgaben mit *a.m.* und *p.m.* kennenlernen.
Wdh: numbers

In the morning

1  Listen and read along.

2 👄 Speak about it in German.

3 👄 Find the rhyme words.

4 👄 Act out the poem.

When I get up in the morning
I jump and listen to the radio sound.
I bend my knees and touch my toes,
I scratch my head and blow my nose.

I wash my face and brush my teeth.
My breakfast is waiting, it's toast and cheese.
After breakfast I get dressed.
Mummy's calling, she sounds stressed:

"Is your school bag packed?
Don't forget your anorak!
You are going to be late!
The school bus will not wait!"

I am off to school
To meet my friends.
That's how my morning ends.

5 👄 Make a poster about your daily routines and present it.

MONDAY	TUESDAY	WEDNESDAY	THURSDAY	FRIDAY	SATURDAY
guitar lessons	Reading Club				SUNDAY

Aufgabe 5: SuS erfragen bei Bedarf unbekannten Wortschatz bei L, schlagen in einem Wörterbuch nach oder verwenden ein Übersetzungsprogramm.

CD 24
KV 28
WB S. 15

seventeen / **17**

Our little town

Interactive map

Places of interest:
press a button

1: town hall
2: market square
3: police station
4: fire station
5: playground
6: toy museum
7: cinema
8: church
9: graveyard
10: hospital
11: fish and
     chip shop
12: post office

1 👄 What can you see in the picture?

2 👂👄 Listen to the dialogue. What is it about?

3 👂 Listen to the audio tour and point.

Eine Wegbeschreibung verstehen.

New words

1 👂👆 Listen and point.

2 👂📖 Listen and read along.

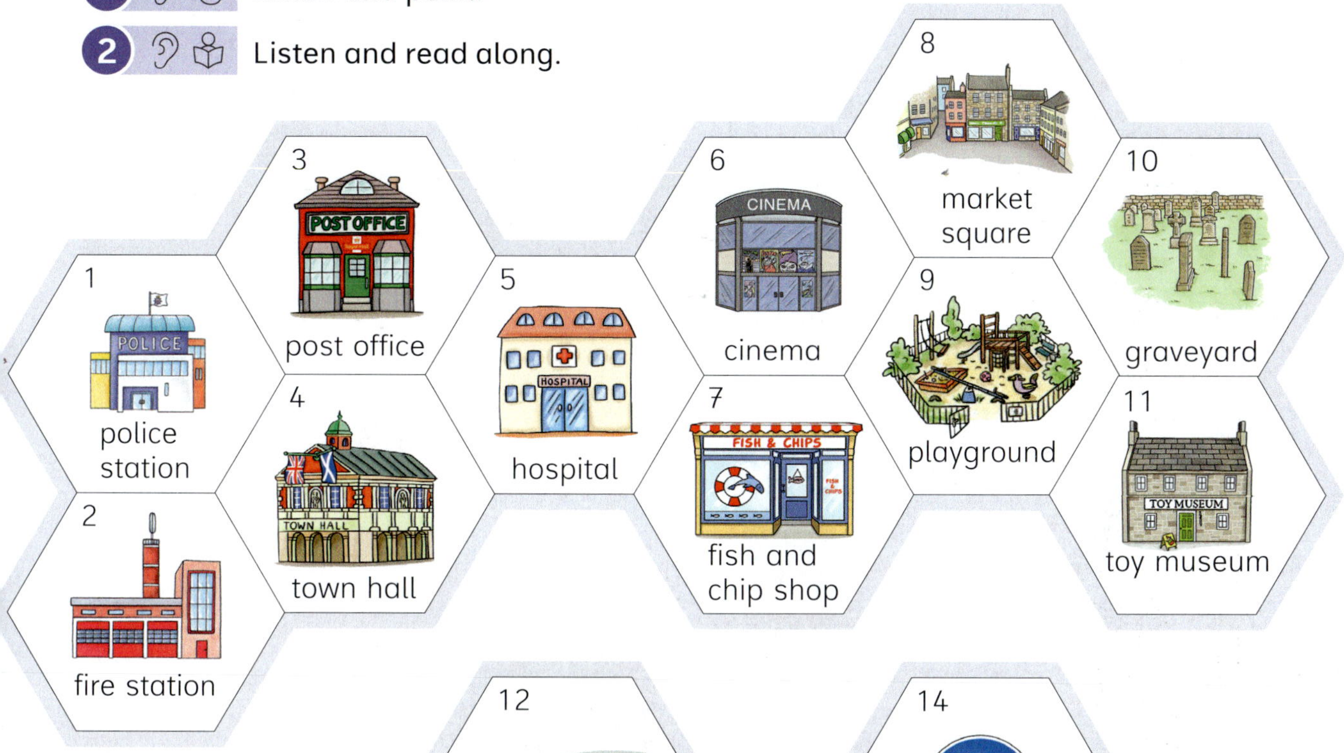

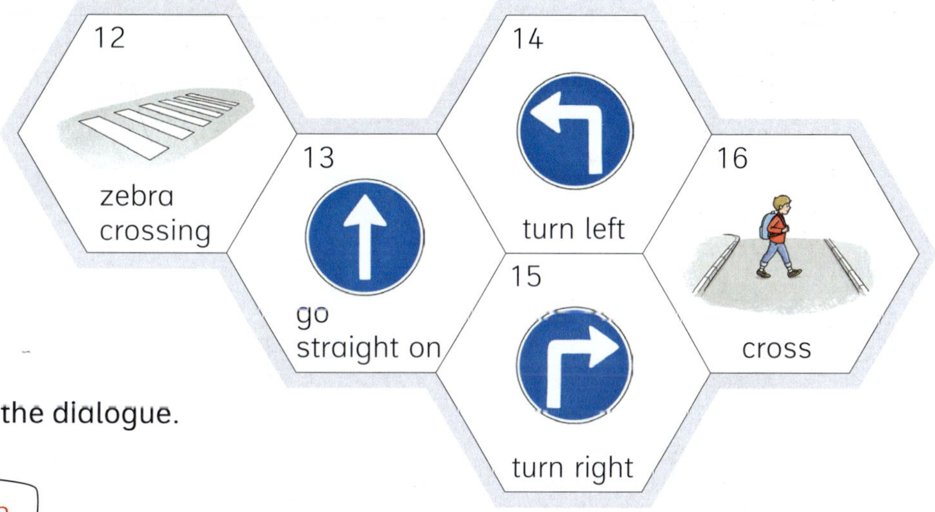

1 police station

2 fire station

3 post office

4 town hall

5 hospital

6 cinema

7 fish and chip shop

8 market square

9 playground

10 graveyard

11 toy museum

12 zebra crossing

13 go straight on

14 turn left

15 turn right

16 cross

3 👥👥👄 Practise the dialogue.

What are you interested in?

I'm interested in the toy museum. What about you?

Sich über interessante Orte in der Stadt austauschen.
Wdh: left, right
Diff ▼ Fö 15–18, **Diff** ▲ Fo 15–18

FC/WC 56–73
CD 29
KV 32–33, 35

 **LET'S TALK!** **Open Day**

OPEN DAY

When? Last Sunday in May
Where? At the police station, toy museum, church
What? Talk to the experts

1 👂 📖 Listen and read along.

2 👀 👄 Practise the dialogue.

I'd like to visit the toy museum.

What would you like to visit?

Because I want to play old games.

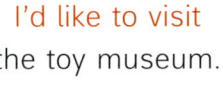

Why?

 talk to a police officer

 sit in a police car

 meet the police dogs

 see the old toys

 play old games

 buy a souvenir

 see the coloured glass windows

 climb the tower

 ring the bells

SuS nehmen ihre Dialoge mit einem Mikrofon auf.
Mit Unterstützung von L kann die Klasse die einzelnen
Aufnahmen zu einem Podcast zusammenstellen.

FC/WC 74–82
CD 33
KV 38

At the toy museum

1   Listen and point.

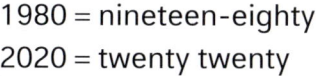
1980 = nineteen-eighty
2020 = twenty twenty

chess
600

Ludo
1869

game console
1995

games

teddy bear
1904

monkey
1950

unicorn
2015

cuddly toys

I like the green car best.
It's from 1967.

Which racing car
do you like best?

What about you?

1920

1967

2020

racing cars

pirate ship
1890

steamboat
1905

motor boat
1990

ships

2 Name the toys.

3 Talk about the toys.

Ein Gespräch über Spielzeuge verstehen.
Sich über die Spielzeuge austauschen.

CD 35
KV 41

twenty-one / 21

At the fish and chip shop

1 👂 👆 Listen and point.

Fish supper..	£6.00
Single fish....	£4.00
Sausage	£2.00
Crisps..........	£1.00

Portions: small | medium | large

	small	medium	large
Chips	£2.00	£2.50	£3.00
Onion rings	£1.50	£2.00	£2.50

Each drink £1.50!

Water
Lemonade
Apple juice
Orange juice

FISH & CHIPS

2 👂 📖 Listen and read along.

David: Can we have two fish suppers, please?
Mr Rossi: Do you want to eat here or do you want a take away?
David: A take away, please.
Mr Rossi: Anything to drink?
David: No, thank you.
Emma: Lemonade, please.
Mr Rossi: Do you want salt and vinegar on your chips?
Emma: No vinegar for me, please. Can I have some tomato ketchup, please?
Mr Rossi: Of course! Here you are. That's 13 pounds and 50 pence.
Emma and David: Thank you! Goodbye, Mr Rossi.

3 👓 Do a role play.

Einen Bestelldialog verstehen. Eigene Dialoge ausdenken und führen. Wdh: numbers, money
Diff ▼ Fö 19, **Diff** ▲ Fo 19

FC/WC 83–96
CD 36, 37
KV 36

Lisa's letter

1 Read Lisa's letter.

Hallo Leute,

letztes Wochenende war ein „bank holiday". Das ist in Großbritannien ein langes Wochenende, bei dem der Montag schulfrei ist. Mir war schrecklich langweilig, alle meine Freunde waren verreist. Mama musste arbeiten und Papa war krank, daher sind wir nicht weggefahren. Meine Freundin Emma hat ihren Cousin David in Schottland besucht. Da hatte sie eine tolle Zeit. Männer im „kilt" hat sie nicht gesehen, nur der „bagpiper" trug einen. David meinte, Kilts würden nur bei besonderen Anlässen wie Hochzeiten getragen. Emma hat ganz viel unternommen und dort die besten „fish and chips" ihres Lebens gegessen. Ihr wisst nicht, was „fish and chips" sind? Das ist in Teig frittierter Fisch mit Pommes. Man isst ihn mit „salt and vinegar", also Salz und Malzessig. Total lecker! Jetzt werde ich ganz hungrig. Mal sehen, was es heute bei uns gibt.

Eure Lisa

TARGET TASK

2 Make a presentation of your favourite place.

Landeskundliches über Schottland erfahren.
Ein Poster gestalten und präsentieren.
SuS können sich bei ihrer Präsentation filmen.

How to do a presentation: S 62
KV 37, 39–40
WB S 20/21

twenty-three / 23

When I grow up

1 👂 ✋ 👄 Listen and point. What is it about?

2 👂 📦 Listen again and read along.

3 📱 Think of your dream job and search the internet.

Einen Vortrag über Polizistinnen und Polizisten verstehen.
Im Internet nach Informationen über Berufe suchen.

CD 40

Jobs

1 Listen and point.

2 Listen and read along.

a builder – an engineer

4 police officer

7 car mechanic

1 builder

5 nurse

2 firefighter

6 bus driver

3 shop assistant

9 zookeeper

8 engineer

10 dentist

11 gardener

12 IT specialist

13 hairdresser

14 office worker

15 farmer

16 teacher

17 waiter/ waitress

3  Practise the dialogue.

What do you want to be?

I want to be an engineer.

Berufsbezeichnungen lernen.
Diff ▼ Fö 20–21, **Diff** ▲ Fo 20–21

FC/WC 97–114
CD 41 **WB** S. 22
KV 42–44

twenty-five / **25**

Lots of jobs

1 🦻 📖 Listen and read along.

2 👄 Guess the jobs.

3 👄 ✊ Find the right photos.

4 👄 Talk about the extra photo.

A

B

Interview 1:

My name is Mary Spencer.
I'm 34 years old.
I have an interesting job.
I love it because I plan and construct
streets and bridges.

C

Interview 2:

Hi, I'm Ron Miller.
I'm 40 years old.
I like my job because I can work
in nature every day.
My favourite plants are roses.

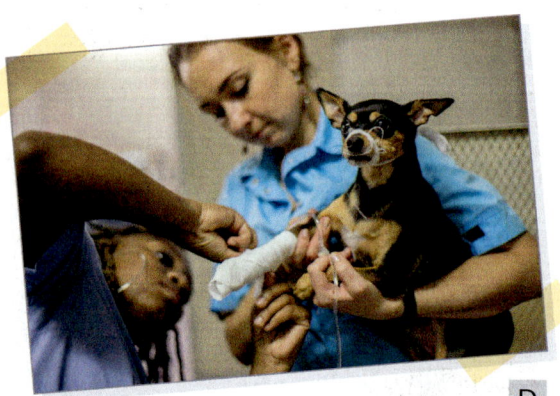

D

Interview 3:

I'm Fred Batson and I'm 47 years old.
My job is never boring because
I meet many people when I drive
through the city.

❯ Ich kann anderen mitteilen, was ich später werden will.

LET'S TALK!   **About my dream job**

1   Listen and point.

2   Listen and read along.

help ill people

sell things

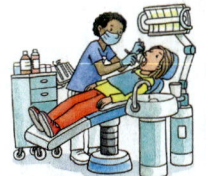

check people's teeth

look after animals

help ill animals

cut hair

build bridges

work with computers

build houses

plant trees and flowers

repair cars

3  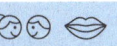   Practise the dialogue.

> What do you want to be when you grow up?

> Why?

> I want to be a firefighter.

> Because I want to help people.

Über Berufswünsche sprechen.
Diff ▼ Fö 22–24, **Diff** ▲ Fo 22–24

FC/WC 116–126
CD 43   **WB** S. 23/24
KV 45–46, 49–51

twenty-seven / **27**

Firefighters in the USA

Hi, I'm Steve Taylor.
I live in the USA.
I'm a firefighter.

1   Listen and point.

2   Listen and read along.

I work in a team in our fire station.
We put out fires, rescue people and teach fire safety.

We wear special clothes
to protect ourselves against fire.

I drive the fire engine.

In very dangerous situations we work with a robot.

3   Speak about it in German.

Einem Sachtext Informationen entnehmen.
Diff ▲ S gibt Detailinformationen auf Deutsch wieder.

CD 44

A firefighter's equipment

1   Listen and point.

> Firefighters have special clothes and equipment to keep them safe from smoke and fire.

lamp — helmet

face shield — air mask

reflective stripes — coat

gloves

axe

pants
trousers

air tank

first-aid kit

rope

water hose

> Firefighters have a face shield.
> They wear a helmet.

2 Describe a firefighter's equipment.

3 Learn the German emergency call number.

112

Germany

999

Great Britain

911

USA

Die Ausrüstung von Feuerwehrleuten beschreiben.
Notrufnummern kennen.

FC/WC 127
CD 45 KV 47–48
WB S. 26

twenty-nine / **29**

Jobs in Great Britain

1  Read Lisa's message. Talk about it.

Neue E-Mail ＿ □ ✕

Von:	lisa@email.co.uk
An:	klasse4a@hummelschule.de
Betreff:	Jobs in Great Britain

Hallo Leute,

in diesem Schuljahr arbeiten wir an einem Projekt über Jobs in Großbritannien. Hier gibt es ganz ausgefallene Berufe wie den *„Ravenmaster"*. Er gehört zu den Wächtern des Tower of London, den *„Beefeaters"*, und kümmert sich besonders um die Raben. In einer Sage heißt es, wenn die Raben aus dem Tower verschwinden, geht das Königreich unter. Interessant, oder? Im Jahr 2007 wurde auch eine Frau erstmals *„Beefeater"* im Tower of London.
Jeff Millers Vater hat auch einen ganz außergewöhnlichen Beruf: Er ist nämlich Butler. Jeff erzählte, dass es für sie eine richtige Schule gibt mit den Unterrichtsfächern Kleider- und Schuhpflege, Servieren und Silberputzen. Jeffs Vater bügelt auch jeden Morgen die Zeitung, damit sein Arbeitgeber keine Druckerschwärze an die Hände bekommt. Darüber musste die ganze Klasse sehr lachen.

Habt ihr auch ein interessantes Projekt?

Eure neugierige Lisa

Senden

Ungewöhnliche britische Berufe kennenlernen.
Sich über den Aufbau einer E-Mail austauschen.

Job presentations

TARGET TASK

1 🗨 Talk about jobs.

> What is your dream job?

> My dream job is to be a builder.
> Builders build houses.
> They like working with tools.

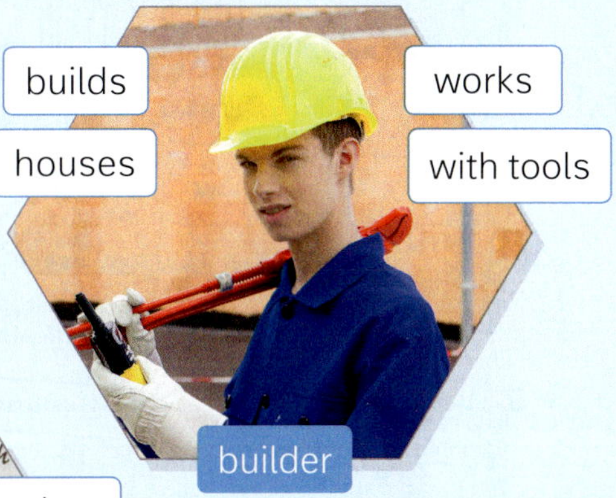

builds
houses
works
with tools
builder

plants
flowers
cuts
grass
gardener

teaches
English
PE
works
at school
teacher

2 ✏️ 🗨 Take notes and do a presentation.

> car mechanics: repair, check, change batteries

Über Berufe sprechen.
Eine Präsentation über einen ausgewählten Beruf halten.

How to do a presentation: S 62
WB S. 27

thirty-one / **31**

Animals

Farm area

Arctic

Antarctic

Watch the
feeding of the …

monkeys at 11.00 a.m.

lions at 12.15 p.m.

goats at 2.30 p.m.

seals and polar bears at 3.15 p.m.

elephant   zebra   giraffe   camel

1 👂🖐 Listen and point.

2 👄 What animals can you see?

3 👄 Plan your day at the zoo.

Sich darüber unterhalten, was man im Zoo machen möchte.
Wdh: time

At the zoo

1  Listen and point.

2  Listen and read along.

1 horse

2 goat

3 pig

4 chicken

5 cow

6 turkey

7 snake

8 polar bear

9 rhino

10 tiger

11 parrot

12 penguin

13 chimpanzee

14 crocodile

15 monkey

16 seal

17 kangaroo

18 hippo

3   Practise the dialogue.

> Which animals would you like to see?

> I'd like to see the seals.

Zoo map

Tiere kennenlernen.
Diff ▼ Fö 25, **Diff** ▲ Fo 25

FC/WC 128–152
CD 48   WB S. 28
KV 52–55

thirty-three / **33**

 **About animals**

1 Read the texts.

Camel
Habitat: desert
Food: plants
Life span: up to
40 years

Chimpanzee
Habitat: jungle
Food: fruit,
plants, meat
Life span: up to
40 years

Cow
Habitat: farm
Food: grass,
hay
Life span: up to
20 years

Chicken
Habitat: farm
Food: grains
Life span: up to
7 years

2 Listen to the children.

3 Practise the dialogue.

4 Talk about the other animals.

Where do chimpanzees live?

What do chimpanzees eat?

Chimpanzees live in the jungle.

Chimpanzees eat fruit, plants and meat.

How long do chimpanzees live?

Chimpanzees live up to 40 years.

Fakten über Tiere erfragen und weitergeben.
Diff ▼ Fö 26–28, **Diff ▲** Fo 26–28

CD 50
KV 56–58, 62–63
WB S. 29

Animals around the world

1   Listen, point and read along.

2   Talk about the animals.

Pandas live in Asia. They are good climbers. They only eat bamboo leaves. They sleep 14 hours a day.

Chimpanzees are noisy and intelligent.

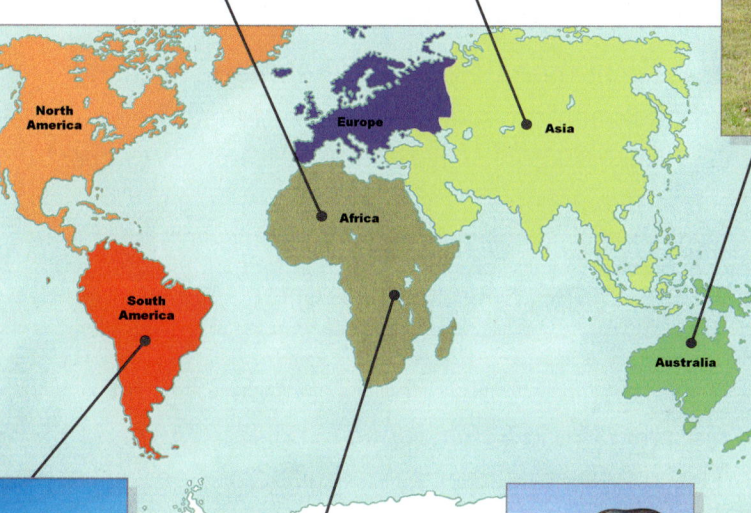

North America

Europe

Asia

Africa

South America

Australia

Antarctic

Kangaroos live in Australia. They can jump high and far. Their babies are born after 38 days. They stay in their mother's pouch to grow.

Penguins live in the Antarctic. They are birds but cannot fly. They lay eggs. The father looks after the babies.

Llamas live in South America. People use their wool. They are good mountain climbers. They spit when they are angry.

Lions live in Africa. They live in groups. You can hear a lion's roar from 5 km away. Lions love to sleep.

Penguins are birds. They are black and white and live in the Antarctic.

Einem Hörtext Informationen entnehmen.
Diff ▼ L liest den Hörtext selbst.
Diff ▲ S gibt Detailinformationen auf Deutsch wieder.

FC/WC 153–160
CD 51

thirty-five / **35**

A chat with Lisa

1 Read Lisa's chat with Anna. Talk about it.

Hey Lisa, was gibt's Neues?

Hi Anna! Ich war gestern im Londoner Zoo. Voll cool!

👍 Hört sich gut an!

Ja, der Zoo ist echt riesig! Es gibt über 700 verschiedene Tiere und man kann dort sogar in kleinen „lodges" übernachten. Nachts kann man dann mit einem „zookeeper" auf Entdeckungstour gehen.

 Wow! Spannend. Hattest du Lieblings-Tiere?

Klaro! 😍 Bei den „feedings", also den Tierfütterungen, hab ich mich ein bisschen in die Schimpansen verliebt. Wusstest du, dass eine bekannte Engländerin namens Jane Goodall sie erforscht hat?

Nein, das wusste ich nicht.

In der Schule sollen wir ein Referat über bekannte Leute halten. Das hat mich auf eine Idee gebracht. 😉

Super! Bin gespannt! See you!

See you!

2   Listen and sing the song Goin' to the zoo.

Informationen über den Londoner Zoo erhalten.
Funktion und Wirkung von Emojis reflektieren.
Den Song Goin' to the zoo singen.

CD 52, 53
KV 59

Jane Goodall

1   Listen to the text and read along.

2 What can you understand? Talk about it in German.

Jane Goodall was born in London in 1934.
She loved animals very much. Her favourite toy was a chimpanzee.
She always wanted to study animals.
But when she finished school she worked as a secretary in London.

One year when she was visiting a friend in Kenya, she met a famous animal researcher.
He asked her to work for him because he was impressed by her knowledge about animals.

They went to Tanzania to study wild chimpanzees.
Jane lived in a tent and tried to get close to them every day.
It took a long time until they let Jane come close.
She gave the chimpanzees names.

All her life Jane Goodall studied the chimpanzees.
She wrote many books about her life with them
and she found out many interesting facts:

→ Chimpanzees eat meat.

→ Chimpanzees use tools for hunting.

→ Chimpanzees show feelings like anger,
happiness and sadness.

TARGET TASK

3 Choose an animal. Find out more interesting facts.
Create your own animal poster.

Einem Text Detailinformationen entnehmen. Im Internet nach
Wissenswertem über Tiere recherchieren und ein Poster gestalten.
Diff ▼ Fö 29, Diff ▲ Fö 29

CD 55
KV 60–61
WB S. 31, 33

thirty-seven / 37

Earth Day

1 👄 What can you see?

2 👂👆 Listen and point.

3 👄 Who is acting green and who is not?

Sich über umweltbewusstes Verhalten austauschen.
Wdh: rooms, furniture, family members

New words

1 👂✋ Listen and point.

2 👂📖 Listen and read along.

1 go by bike

2 take public transport

3 switch on/off

4 save water

5 save energy

6 save petrol

7 collect rubbish

8 buy second hand

9 repair things

10 recycle paper

11 newspapers

12 cans

13 batteries

14 broken glass

15 plastic wrappings

16 Don't waste food!

3 👀👄 Practise the dialogue.

What can we do to save nature?

We can go to school by bike.

We can save water.

Sagen, was man Positives für die Umwelt tun kann.
Diff ▼ Fö 30–31, **Diff** ▲ Fo 30–31

FC/WC 161–178
CD 57 **WB** S. 34
KV 64–65

thirty-nine / **39**

 **About a graph**

1   Listen and point.

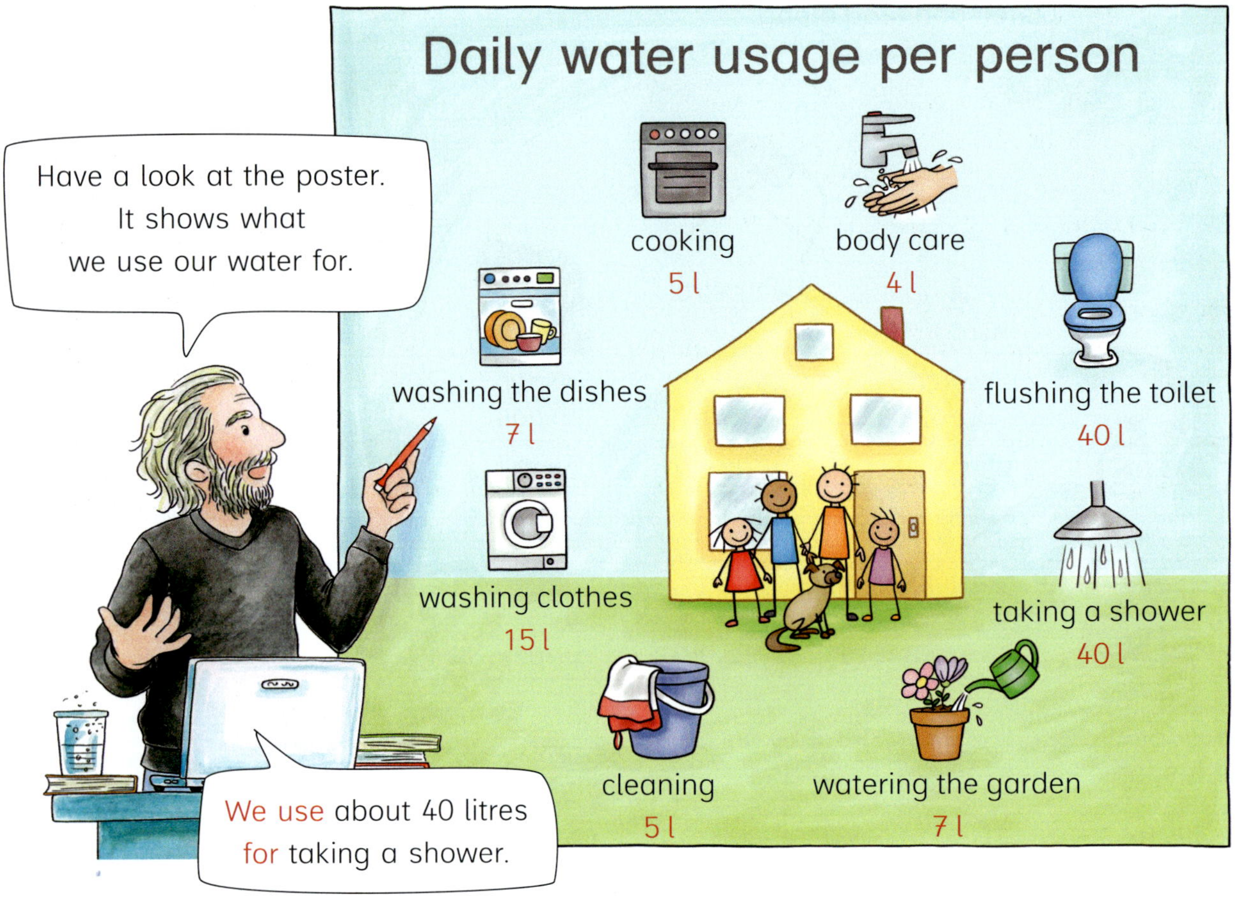

> Have a look at the poster. It shows what we use our water for.

Daily water usage per person

cooking
5 l

body care
4 l

washing the dishes
7 l

flushing the toilet
40 l

washing clothes
15 l

taking a shower
40 l

cleaning
5 l

watering the garden
7 l

> We use about 40 litres for taking a shower.

2  Listen and read along.

3  Talk about the poster.

> How much water do we use for washing the dishes?

> We use 7 litres for washing the dishes.

Song: With my own two hands

1 🎧 Listen to the song.

2 🎧 📖 Listen and read along.

I can change the world, with my own two hands.
Make it a better place, with my own two hands.
Make it a kinder place, with my own two hands.
With my own, with my own two hands.

I can make peace on earth, with my own two hands.
I can clean up the earth, with my own two hands.
I can reach out to you, with my own two hands.
With my own, with my own two hands.
With my own, with my own two hands.

I'm gonna make it a brighter place, (with my own two hands).
I'm gonna make it a safer place, (with my own two hands).
I'm gonna help the human race, (with my own two hands).
With my own, with my own two hands.
With my own, with my own two hands.

Lyrics: Ben C. Harper

3 👄 What do you understand? Talk in German.

Ich kann die Welt verändern, mit meinen eigenen Händen.

Einen freundlicheren Ort machen, mit meinen eigenen beiden Händen.

Charity shops

1  Read Lisa's blog post. Talk about it.

2 Compare to your countries.

LISA IN GREAT BRITAIN

Hi guys,

ich komme gerade vom Einkaufen in einem „*charity shop*". Dort hab ich mir Lesestoff gekauft – eine ganze Tüte voll! Da staunt ihr wohl, wie ich das mit meinem Taschengeld schaffe? In den „*charity shops*" werden nämlich Bücher, Kleidung und alle möglichen Sachen für ganz wenig Geld verkauft. Diese Sachen haben Leute dem Laden geschenkt, weil sie sie nicht einfach wegwerfen wollen. Der Gewinn geht an eine gute Sache, zum Beispiel an Organisationen, die gegen Krebs kämpfen oder die sich für Kinderprojekte einsetzen. So habe ich schöne Bücher günstig bekommen und noch etwas Gutes für die Umwelt getan! Übrigens hab ich dort eine Vase wieder gesehen, die wir beim Parkputzen gefunden haben. Klasse, was?

Bis bald, Lisa

SuS analysieren und reflektieren Funktion und Bedeutung von Blogs, auch im Vergleich zu Webseiten.

Celebrating Earth Day

1   Listen and read along.

2   Explain in German what Earth Day is.

The first **Earth Day** was more than 50 years ago.
Every year people around the world celebrate Earth Day on the **22nd** of **April**.
They want to show that we have to **protect our planet**.
Every year they meet for discussions, demonstrations and activities.

People in Australia also started to celebrate an **Earth Hour** in 2007.
More than 2 million people **switched off their lights.**
They wanted to show that we can save energy **when we all work together**.

TARGET TASK

3   Read the poster. What is it about?

4 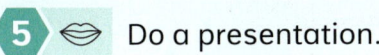 Create a poster for the next Earth Day.

5 Do a presentation.

SAVE OUR PLANET

Go to school by bike and NOT by car!

Recycle and Repair! Don't throw away!

Buy second hand

SECOND HAND SHOP

VOLUNTEER

Go shopping and save money!
Reuse nice clothes, bikes, toys and computers.
Say yes to second hand!

Einem Sachtext Detailinformationen entnehmen.
Ein eigenes Poster zum *Earth Day* gestalten und präsentieren.
Diff ▼ Fö 32, **Diff** ▲ Fo 32

FC/WC 187
CD 62   WB S. 39
KV 66–71

forty-three / 43

Fred, the super dog

It's Earth Day today – a day to help nature. That's why Ben and Ravi meet with some people to clean up the park. A lady from the "Help our earth club" welcomes them and gives them bags for collecting rubbish.

Ben and Ravi take Fred to the playground. They find a lot of plastic wrappings and put them into the yellow bag.

Fred brings a plastic bottle from under the bush. Ben and Ravi laugh and thank Fred for his help.

Eine Geschichte verstehen und nachspielen.
Diff ▼ L liest die Geschichte selbst.
Diff ▲ S gibt den Inhalt der Story auf Deutsch wieder.

CD 65
SC 11–17
Fö/Fo 33

Fred finds an old newspaper under the slide. The boys put it into the paper bag.

Suddenly Fred starts barking. He is very worried. The boys don't know what's going on.

Ben and Ravi go closer.
Now they know why Fred is so worried.
A hedgehog is stuck in an old can and can't get out!

Now the boys are worried too.
How can they help the poor hedgehog?
What can they do?

1 👂 📖 Listen to the story and read along.

2 👄 Talk about the story in German.

A

B

3 📖 👂 Choose one of the endings (A or B) and listen to it.

4 👓 Do a role play.

How to do a role play: S. 63

What can you see in the pictures?
Why is Fred worried?
What would you do to help the hedgehog?

CD 66, 67
KV 72

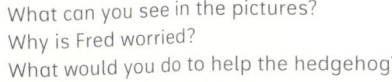

Holidays

1 👂👆 Listen and point.

2 👄 What do you want to do at the beach?

Eine Strandszene beschreiben.

New words

1 👂👆 Listen and point.

2 👂📖 Listen and read along.

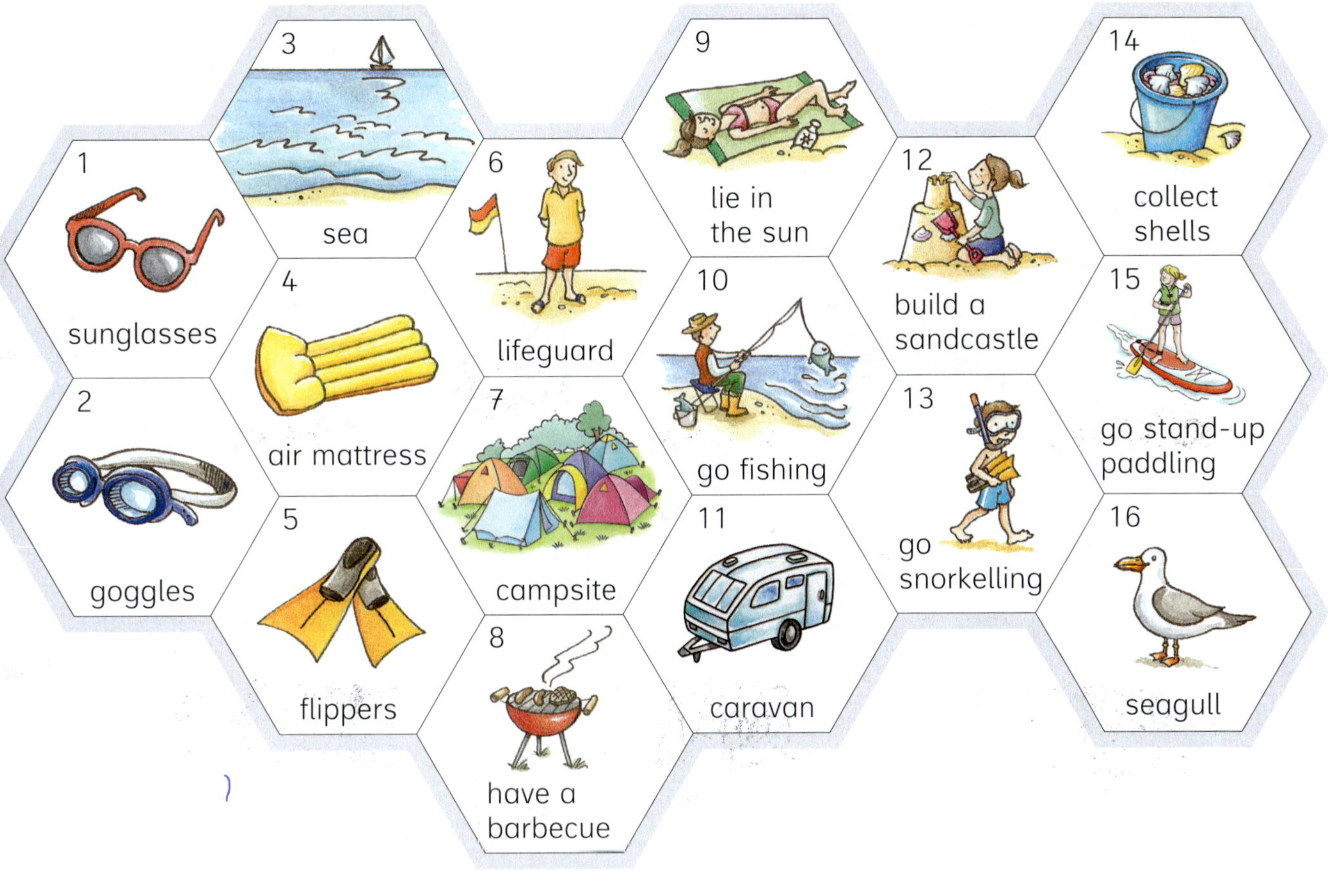

3 sea

1 sunglasses

4 air mattress

2 goggles

5 flippers

6 lifeguard

7 campsite

8 have a barbecue

9 lie in the sun

10 go fishing

11 caravan

12 build a sandcastle

13 go snorkelling

14 collect shells

15 go stand-up paddling

16 seagull

3 👥👄 Practise the dialogue.

Let's collect shells.

Yes, great idea!

No, let's go stand-up paddling.

Einen Vorschlag machen. Diesen annehmen oder ablehnen.
Diff ▼ Fö 35 **Diff** ▲ Fo 35

FC/WC 188–203
CD 69 WB S. 40
KV 73–74

forty-seven / 47

 **LET'S TALK!** **What are you going to do?**

1 Listen and point.

have a barbecue

go fishing

play beach volleyball

lie in the sun

go snorkelling

have a campfire

go stand-up paddling

collect shells

go slacklining

go swimming

2 Read the dialogue.

3 Do a role play.

What are you going to do today?

I'm going to go snorkelling. In the evening we are going to have a barbecue.

Diff ▼ Fö 36–37, Diff ▲ Fo 36–37
SuS schlagen weitere mögliche Aktivitäten in einem
analogen oder digitalen Wörterbuch nach.

FC/WC 197–207
CD 70   WB S. 41
KV 75, 78, 80, 82

Coconut cream rap

  1 Listen to the rap and speak along.

Text nach Frank Leto

> Cream your hands – I cream my hands,
> cream your elbows – I cream my elbows,
> cream your arms – I cream my arms,
> with coconut cream – with coconut cream.
>
> Cream your face – I cream my face,
> cream your neck – I cream my neck,
> cream your shoulders – I cream my shoulders,
> with coconut cream – with coconut cream.
>
> Protect my eyes with glasses, protect my head with a hat,
> and when I want to protect my skin – I cream my body with coconut cream.

 2 Talk about Lisa's letter.

Hallo ihr!

Wusstet ihr schon, dass viele Engländer das Wochenende auf einem Dauercampingplatz verbringen? Auch Bens Familie fährt oft zum „camping" an die englische Südküste. An britischen Stränden gibt es immer eine Station der „Royal National Lifeboat Institution", die man in Deutschland unter dem Namen DLRG (Deutsche Lebens-Rettungs-Gesellschaft) kennt. Mitglied kann man hier erst mit 17 werden. Aber für Kinder gibt es den „Storm Force Club". Da trifft man sich regelmäßig und erfährt alles über sicheres Verhalten am Strand und im Wasser.

Eure Lisa

Einen Rap sprechen. Wdh: body parts
Landeskundliches über Camping in England erfahren.
Diff ▼ Fö 34, **Diff** ▲ Fo 34

CD 72, 73
KV 76–77, 81

forty-nine / **49**

Campsite rules

1  Listen and point.

2 Read the rules and match the pictures.

3 Do a role play.

Campsite rules

No cars on the campsite.
No noise between 12 p.m. and
3 p.m., and after 10 p.m.
Don't play ball games between
the caravans.
Keep your dog on a lead.
Dog owners must clean up
after their dogs.
Do not feed the seagulls.

Regeln auf einem Campingplatz verstehen
und begründen.

A holiday story

1   Listen and point.

2 Talk about the story in German.

3 Choose a title.

> A: A nice barbecue in the evening
> B: A barbecue for the seagulls
> C: The seagull attack

Eine Bildergeschichte verstehen.
Diff ▲ S gibt Inhalt der Story auf Deutsch wieder.
Target task: WB S. 44

SC 18–21
CD 76   WB S. 44/45
KV 79

fifty-one / 51

The first Thanksgiving

pilgrims

America

ship

Native Americans

corn

turkey

In 1620 about 100  sailed from England to  on their

called Mayflower. It was a hard trip to . They landed at Plymouth Rock

in December 1620. The first winter was very cold. The  helped to build houses.

In spring they showed the  how to plant , hunt and catch fish.

In autumn the  were very thankful and invited the  to come

to a big meal and eat . This was the first Thanksgiving.

1   Listen and read along.

2   What can you understand? Talk about it in German.

Den Ursprung des Thanksgiving-Festes erfahren.
Diff ▼ Landeskundliche Informationen auf Deutsch geben.

FC/WC 220–226
CD 78
KV 83

Thanksgiving today

1 Look at the photos and read the text.

2 What is the text about?

3 Do you know other festivals like Thanksgiving?

Thanksgiving is a traditional holiday in the USA. It's on the fourth Thursday in November.
On this day, families get together. Sons, daughters, grandparents, uncles, aunts and
cousins meet and have a nice meal.
The traditional food is turkey, potatoes, pumpkin and corn.
There is a big Thanksgiving parade in New York. It lasts for three hours.
More than 3 million people visit the parade. About 50 million people watch it live on TV.
They want to see the marching bands and dancing cheerleaders.
There are big balloons showing cartoon characters.
In the afternoon, many families watch American football on TV.
The next day is called Black Friday and many people go shopping.

Landeskundliche Informationen zu Thanksgiving erhalten.
Sich über ähnliche Festlichkeiten in anderen Ländern austauschen.
Diff ▼ Fö 38, **Diff** ▲ Fo 38

FC/WC 227–228
KV 84
WB S. 46

fifty-three / **53**

The story of St Patrick

1 🦻 📖 Listen and read along.

2 👄 Talk about the story in German.

1600 years ago, when Patrick was 16 years old, Irish pirates kidnapped him from his family in England.

He worked as a slave on an Irish farm.

After 6 years he escaped from Ireland and became a priest.

Many years later, Patrick went back to Ireland to tell people about God.

A famous legend says that Patrick chased all the snakes out of Ireland.

He used the shamrock to tell people about the Holy Trinity: Father, Son, Holy Spirit.

Eine Bildergeschichte über die Legende zu Sankt Patrick verstehen.

SC 22–27
CD 79

St Patrick's Day

1 Read Lisa's letter.

2 Read the rhyme and learn it by heart.

Dia duit (so begrüßt man sich in Irland),

gestern war ich bei meinem Klassenkameraden Aiden eingeladen. Seine Familie kommt aus Irland und wir haben gemeinsam „Saint Patrick's Day" gefeiert. Saint Patrick war ein Heiliger und er lebte in Irland. Er hat den Menschen von Gott erzählt. Wir haben uns grüne Sachen angezogen und Aiden hat für uns alle grüne Hüte mitgebracht. Bei ihm war alles mit Kleeblättern (dem Erkennungszeichen von Saint Patrick) geschmückt. Es gab dann auch nur Grünes zu essen und zu trinken und wir haben im Fernsehen die „Saint Patrick's Day parade" in Chicago angeschaut. Da war richtig was los. Es spielten Musikgruppen, es wurde getanzt und alle sahen dabei sehr fröhlich aus. Stellt euch vor, sie haben sogar den Fluss („river") mit Lebensmittelfarbe grün gefärbt.

Slán (das heißt Tschüss auf Irisch),
Lisa

A leprechaun is small and green.
He hides where he cannot be seen.
But if you catch one this very day,
He must give his gold away.

Informationen über den St Patrick's Day erhalten. Einen Reim auswendig lernen und vortragen. SuS können sich beim Vortrag filmen.
Diff ▼ Fö 39, **Diff** ▲ Fo 39

FC/WC   229–232
KV   85

fifty-five / **55**

The story of the leprechaun

1 👂 📖 Listen to the story and read along.

2 👄 Talk about the story in German.

3 👂 👄 Listen to the Leprechaun song and sing along.

4 👓 Do a role play.

One day a young man walked through a forest in Ireland.
Suddenly he heard the tap-tapping of a small hammer.

It came from a leprechaun who was repairing a shoe.

The man knew that leprechauns have a pot of gold. So he grabbed the leprechaun and asked, "Where is your pot of gold?"

Eine mythologische Figur kennenlernen.
Diff ▾ L liest die Geschichte selbst.
Diff ▴ Die Geschichte mit verteilten Rollen nachspielen.

CD 80–82
SC 28–35

The leprechaun said,
"The pot of gold ... eh ... is ... eh ...
over there, under the bush."

The man marked the bush with his red scarf.

"Don't take my scarf away!",
he said to the leprechaun.

The man ran home to get a spade.
The leprechaun was left behind.

When the man came back with his spade, the leprechaun was gone.
But there was a red scarf on every bush in the forest.
Poor man – the leprechaun had played a trick on him.

Do you believe in leprechauns?
Why are there so many red scarves?
Do you think the man will find the pot of gold?

How to do a role play: S. 63
WB S. 47
KV 86

Fit for 5!

1 👂 👆 Listen and point.

2 🎲 Play the game.

⚀ Give me five words.   ⚁ Make an odd-one-out.   ⚂ Describe the picture.

Themen der Lernjahre wiederholen. Ein Bild aussuchen, würfeln.
Den Auftrag der Würfelzahl ausführen. Auf dem Bumblebee card-
Feld werden die Kärtchen von KV 90 und 91 platziert.

CD 88

5

Bumblebee card

6

7

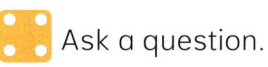 Ask a question.　　 Do a role play.　　 Take a Bumblebee card.

How to write

Ich überlege mir, was
ich schreiben möchte.

My favourite
animals are …

Ich vergleiche
mein Geschriebenes
mit der Vorlage.

**Das hilft mir beim
Schreiben.**

Ich erinnere mich an die
passenden Wörter und
Sätze.

Ich frage meine Lehrkraft.

Ich suche nach
einer Schreibvorlage in
meinem Textbook
oder Workbook.

Ich schlage in einem Wörterbuch nach
oder spreche meine Frage in ein
Übersetzungsprogramm im Internet hinein.

How to check my texts

Ich schreibe **I** (ich) immer groß.

Ich benutze im Englischen keine Umlaute (kein ä / ö / ü).

Ich bitte ein Partnerkind, sich meinen Text einmal genau durchzulesen und einen Kommentar zu geben.

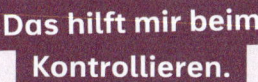

Das hilft mir beim Kontrollieren.

table

Ich denke daran, dass man im Englischen nicht immer so schreibt wie man spricht.

Ich schreibe Namen, Wochentage und Monate immer groß.

Ich schreibe Satzanfänge groß.

How to do a presentation

Ich sammle und ordne
Stichwörter zum Thema
in einer Mindmap.

Ich suche Bilder oder
Gegenstände, mit denen ich
alles gut verdeutlichen kann.

**Das hilft mir beim
Erstellen einer Präsentation.**

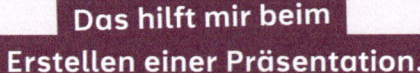

Beim Vortragen schaue
ich das Publikum an
und versuche frei und
deutlich zu sprechen.

Wenn ich meine Präsentation
anfertige, achte ich auf einfache
Sätze und eine deutliche Schrift.

Wenn mir ein Wort während der
Präsentation nicht einfällt, zeige ich
es auf einem der ausgewählten Bilder
oder stelle es pantomimisch dar.

Ich übe
meinen Vortrag.

How to do a role play

Wir spielen das Theaterstück den anderen Kindern vor und fragen nach ihrer Meinung.

Wir suchen uns eine Geschichte aus, in der es für mehrere Kinder eine Rolle gibt.

Wir üben das Theaterstück Szene für Szene. Alle erhalten eine bestimmte Aufgabe, damit z.B. das Bühnenbild stimmt und Musik oder Geräusche eingespielt werden.

Das hilft mir beim Vorbereiten eines Rollenspiels

Wir suchen alle Texte zusammen, die wir schon für die Geschichte haben.

Wir üben die Texte und verteilen dann die Rollen. Wir überlegen, welche Verkleidung oder Requisiten wir brauchen.

Manchmal müssen wir noch zusätzliche Rollentexte oder das Ende der Geschichte schreiben. Dabei kann unsere Lehrkraft uns helfen.

Wir hören uns Musterdialoge auf der CD an.

Look it up!

A B C D E F G H I J K L M N O P Q R S T U V W X Y Z

A

about	über
accident	der Unfall
act out	spielen, vorführen
action	die Aktion
activity	die Aktivität
afternoon	der Nachmittag
again	wieder, noch einmal
age	das Alter
air mask	die Atemschutzmaske
air mattress	die Luftmatratze
air tank	die Sauerstoffflasche
all	alle
anger	der Ärger
angry	verärgert
animal	das Tier
anorak	die Windjacke
answer	die Antwort, antworten
Antarctic	die Antarktis
apple juice	der Apfelsaft
Arctic	die Arktis
area	der Bereich
arm	der Arm
around	um, herum
arrest	festnehmen, verhaften
Art	der Kunstunterricht
Asia	Asien
asleep	schlafend
Assembly	die Versammlung
assistant	der Assistent, die Assistentin
at	an, bei, um, in
attack	der Angriff
aunt	die Tante
Australia	Australien
autumn	der Herbst
axe	die Axt

B

back	der Rücken, zurück
bag	der Beutel, die Tüte
ball game	das Ballspiel
balloon	der Ballon
bamboo leaves	Bambusblätter
barbecue	der Grill, grillen
bark	bellen
battery	die Batterie
beach	der Strand
because	weil
bed	das Bett
behind	hinter, zurück
bell	die Glocke
bend	beugen
between	zwischen
big	groß
bike	das Fahrrad
bin	der Abfalleimer
bird	der Vogel
birthday party	die Geburtstagsfeier
blink	blinken
blow my nose	meine Nase putzen
body	der Körper
body care	die Körperpflege
book	das Buch
boring	langweilig
born	geboren
bottle	die Flasche
break	die Pause
breakfast	das Frühstück
bridge	die Brücke
bright	hell
broken	zerbrochen, kaputt
brother	der Bruder
brush	bürsten, putzen
build	bauen
builder	der Bauarbeiter, die Bauarbeiterin
bump	zusammenstoßen
bus driver	der Busfahrer, die Busfahrerin
bush	der Busch
buy	kaufen

C

call	rufen
camel	das Kamel
camping	campen
campfire	das Lagerfeuer
campsite	der Campingplatz
can	die Dose
Canada	Kanada
car mechanic	der Automechaniker, die Automechanikerin
caravan	der Wohnwagen
card	die Karte
catch	fangen
celebrate	feiern
change	verändern
chase	verfolgen
check	überprüfen
cheese	der Käse
chicken	das Hühnchen
child	das Kind
children	die Kinder
chimpanzee	der Schimpanse
chips	die Pommes frites
choose	aussuchen
church	die Kirche
cinema	das Kino
city	die Stadt
class	die Klasse
clean	sauber, putzen
clean up	sauber machen
clever	schlau
climb	klettern
clock	Uhr
close	nah
clothes	die Kleidung
coastline	die Küste
coconut	die Kokosnuss
cold	kalt
collect	sammeln
colour	die Farbe, anmalen
coloured	farbig, bunt

construct	bauen, errichten
cook	kochen
corn	der Mais
count	zählen
country	das Land
cousin	der Cousin, die Cousine
cow	die Kuh
Crafts	der Werkunterricht
cream	die Creme, eincremen
crisps	die Chips
criminal	der Verbrecher, die Verbrecherin
crocodile	das Krokodil
cross	überqueren
cut	schneiden

D

daily	täglich
dance	tanzen
danger	die Gefahr
dangerous	gefährlich
daughter	die Tochter
day	der Tag
dentist	der Zahnarzt, die Zahnärztin
demonstration	die Demonstration
describe	beschreiben
desert	die Wüste
different	unterschiedlich
dinner	das Abendessen
direction	die Richtung
dirty	schmutzig
discussion	die Diskussion
dishes	das Geschirr
dog	der Hund
draw	zeichnen
dream	der Traum, träumen
drink	das Getränk, trinken
drive	fahren

A B C D E F G H I J K L M N O P Q R S T U V W X Y Z

E

earth . . . . .die Erde
Earth Day. . . . . .Tag der Erde
eat. . . . . .essen
egg . . . . .das Ei
elephant. . . . . .der Elefant
elbow. . . . . .der Ellbogen
emergency. . . . . .der Notfall
end . . . . .das Ende, beenden,
                            enden
energy. . . . . .die Energie
engineer . . . . .der Ingenieur,
                            die Ingenieurin
English . . . . .Englisch,
                            der Englischunterricht
equipment . . . . .die Ausrüstung
evening. . . . . .der Abend
every . . . . .jeder, jede, jedes
excited. . . . . .aufgeregt
excuse me . . . . .Entschuldigung

F

face . . . . .das Gesicht
face shield . . . . .der Gesichtsschutz
fact . . . . .die Tatsache
family. . . . . .die Familie
famous . . . . .berühmt
far . . . . .weit
farm . . . . .der Bauernhof
farmer . . . . .der Bauer, die Bäuerin
fast . . . . .schnell
father. . . . . .der Vater
favourite . . . . .lieblings
feather . . . . .die Feder
feed . . . . .füttern
feeding . . . . .die Fütterung
feeling. . . . . .das Gefühl
feet . . . . .die Füße
find . . . . .finden
fine . . . . .gut
fire. . . . . .das Feuer
fire engine . . . . .das Feuerwehrauto

fire station . . . . .die Feuerwache
firefighter . . . . .der Feuerwehrmann,
                            die Feuerwehrfrau
first . . . . .erster, erste, erstes
first-aid kit . . . . .der Erste-Hilfe-Kasten
fish . . . . .der Fisch
fishing . . . . .fischen
flag . . . . .die Flagge
flippers . . . . .die Flossen
flower . . . . .die Blume
flush . . . . .spülen
fly . . . . .fliegen
food . . . . .das Essen
foot . . . . .der Fuß
forest . . . . .der Wald
forget . . . . .vergessen
free. . . . . .frei
friend . . . . .der Freund,
                            die Freundin
from . . . . .aus
fruit. . . . . .Obst
fun. . . . . .der Spaß
future. . . . . .die Zukunft

G

game . . . . .das Spiel
garden. . . . . .der Garten
gardener. . . . . .der Gärtner,
                            die Gärtnerin
German. . . . . .Deutsch,
                            der Deutschunterricht
Germany. . . . . .Deutschland
get dressed . . . . .sich anziehen
get out. . . . . .herauskommen
get up . . . . .aufstehen
giraffe . . . . .die Giraffe
glass . . . . .das Glas
glasses . . . . .die Brille
gloves . . . . .die Handschuhe
goat . . . . .die Ziege
God. . . . . .Gott
goggles . . . . .die Taucherbrille

gold .... das Gold
Golden Time .... die Freiarbeitszeit
grab .... greifen, packen
grains .... das Getreide
grandparents .... die Großeltern
grass .... das Gras
graveyard .... der Friedhof
Great Britain .... Großbritannien
group .... die Gruppe

H

habitat .... der Lebensraum
hair .... das Haar
hairdresser .... der Friseur,
                      die Friseurin
hammer .... der Hammer
hand .... die Hand
happiness .... die Freude
hat .... der Hut
hay .... das Heu
head .... der Kopf
hedgehog .... der Igel
helmet .... der Helm
help .... die Hilfe, helfen
hide .... verstecken
high .... hoch
hippo .... das Nilpferd
hobby .... das Hobby
holiday .... der Feiertag,
                     der Urlaub, die Ferien
Holy Trinity .... die Heilige
                      Dreieinigkeit
Holy Spirit .... Heiliger Geist
homework .... die Hausaufgabe
hospital .... das Krankenhaus
hour .... die Stunde
horns .... die Hörner
how .... wie
human race .... die Menschheit
hungry .... hungrig
hunt .... jagen

I

ice hockey .... das Eishockey
ICT .... der Informatik-
                     unterricht
idea .... die Idee
if .... falls
ill .... krank
important .... wichtig
impressed .... beeindruckt
in .... in
in front of .... vor
India .... Indien
intelligent .... intelligent
interested .... interessiert
interview .... das Interview
into .... in, in ... hinein
invite .... einladen
Ireland .... Irland
Irish .... Irisch
island .... die Insel
IT specialist .... der Computer-
                      Fachmann, die
                      Computer-Fachfrau

J

jacket .... die Jacke
job .... der Job
join in .... mitmachen
jump .... springen
jungle .... der Dschungel

K

kangaroo .... das Känguru
key .... der Schlüssel
kind .... freundlich
knee .... das Knie
know .... wissen
knowledge .... das Wissen

L

label..................beschriften
lake..................der See
language ....die Sprache
large.................groß
last ....letzter, letzte, letztes
late ....spät
laugh ....lachen
lay ....legen
lead ....die Hundeleine
learn.................lernen
learn it by heart.......auswendig lernen
leave ....etwas lassen,
                    jemanden verlassen
left...................links
leg...................das Bein
legend ....die Legende
lemonade...........die Limonade
leprechaun ....der Kobold
letter ....der Brief
library ....die Bibliothek
lie in the sun ....in der Sonne liegen
life span ....die Lebensdauer
light ....das Licht
like ....mögen
lion ....der Löwe
list...................die Liste
listen to..............zuhören
litre ....der Liter
live ....leben
love..................die Liebe, lieben
lunch ....das Mittagessen
lunch break..........die Mittagspause

M

mane ....die Mähne
map ....die Landkarte
marching band ......die Blaskapelle
mark.................markieren
market square ....der Marktplatz
Maths ....der Mathematik-
                    unterricht

N

meal.................die Mahlzeit
meat.................das Fleisch
medium.............hier: mittelgroß
meet.................treffen
menu ....die Speisekarte
milk..................die Milch
miss ....fehlen
moment ....der Moment
monkey ....der Affe
month ....der Monat
morning ....der Morgen
much ....viel
museum ....das Museum
Music...............der Musikunterricht
my...................mein, meine, mein

nasty ....böse, gemein
Native Americans .....Urbevölkerung
                    Amerikas
nature ....die Natur
near ....nahe
neck ....der Hals
new.................neu
newspaper ....die Zeitung
next ....nächster, nächste,
                    nächstes
next to ....neben
noisy ....laut
number ....die Nummer,
                    nummerieren
nurse ....die Krankenschwester,
                    der Krankenpfleger

O

office worker.........der Büroangestellte,
                    die Büroangestellte
old...................alt
on ....auf, an, bei
onion ring...........der Zwiebelring
only.................nur
open................geöffnet, öffnen

open day	der Tag der offenen Tür
orange juice	der Orangensaft
over	über
owner	der Besitzer, die Besitzerin

P

pack	packen
panda	der Pandabär
paper	das Papier
parade	die Parade
parrot	der Papagei
pay	bezahlen
PE	der Sportunterricht
peace	der Frieden
penguin	der Pinguin
people	die Menschen
petrol	das Benzin
photo	das Foto
picture	das Bild
pilgrim	der Pilger, die Pilgerin
pirate	der Pirat, die Piratin
place	der Platz, der Ort
plan	der Plan, planen
planet	der Planet
plant	die Pflanze
plastic	das Plastik
plate	der Teller
play	spielen
playground	der Spielplatz
please	bitte
poem	das Gedicht
point to	auf etwas zeigen
polar bear	der Eisbär
police car	das Polizeiauto
police officer	der Polizist, die Polizistin
police station	die Polizeiwache
pond	der Teich
poor	arm
portion	die Portion
post office	das Postamt

poster	das Poster
pot	der Topf
potato	die Kartoffel
pouch	der Beutel
practise	üben
presentation	die Präsentation
priest	der Priester, die Priesterin
problem	das Problem
project	das Projekt
protect	schützen
public	öffentlich
pumpkin	der Kürbis
put on	anziehen
put out	(Feuer) löschen
pyjamas	der Schlafanzug

Q

quarter past	Viertel nach
quarter to	Viertel vor

R

race	das Rennen
radio	das Radio
read	lesen
recycle	wiederverwerten
repair	reparieren
researcher	der Forscher, die Forscherin
rhino	das Nashorn
rhyme	der Reim, reimen
right	rechts, richtig
ring	der Ring, läuten
roar	brüllen
robot	der Roboter
role play	das Rollenspiel
room	der Raum
rope	das Seil
rose	die Rose
rubbish	der Müll
rule	die Regel
run	rennen

A B C D E F G H I J K L M N O P Q R S T U V W X Y Z

S

sadness	die Traurigkeit
safe	sicher
sail	segeln
salt	das Salz
sandcastle	die Sandburg
sausage	das Würstchen
save	sparen, retten
scarf	der Schal
school	die Schule
Science	der Sachunterricht
Scotland	Schottland
scratch	kratzen
sea	das Meer
seal	der Seehund
seagull	die Möwe
secretary	der Sekretär, die Sekretärin
sentence	der Satz
shamrock	das Kleeblatt
shell	die Muschel
ship	das Schiff
shoe	der Schuh
shop assistant	der Verkäufer, die Verkäuferin
shoulder	die Schulter
show	zeigen
shower	die Dusche
sing	singen
sister	die Schwester
sit	sitzen
situation	die Situation
skin	die Haut
slacklining	auf einem Seil balancieren
slave	der Sklave, die Sklavin
slide	die Rutsche
small	klein
smoke	der Rauch
snake	die Schlange
snorkel	schnorcheln

solution	die Lösung
son	der Sohn
sound	der Klang
South Africa	Südafrika
South America	Südamerika
souvenir	das Souvenir
spade	der Spaten
speak	sprechen
special	besonders
spit	spucken
spring	der Frühling
start	anfangen
stop	aufhören
story	die Geschichte
straight ahead	geradeaus
street	die Straße
stressed	gestresst
study	studieren, untersuchen
subject	das Unterrichtsfach
sunglasses	die Sonnenbrille
swim	schwimmen
switch on/off	anschalten/ ausschalten

T

tail	der Schwanz
take	nehmen
take a shower	duschen
take away	zum Mitnehmen
teacher	die Lehrkraft
teeth	die Zähne
telephone	das Telefon
tell	erzählen
tent	das Zelt
terrible	schrecklich
thank	danken
thankful	dankbar
Thanksgiving	(vgl. mit) Erntedank- fest
thing	das Ding, die Sache
through	durch

tidy	. . . .	aufgeräumt, sauber
tiger	. . . .	der Tiger
timetable	. . . .	der Stundenplan
tired	. . . .	müde
today	. . . .	heute
toes	. . . .	Zehen
together	. . . .	zusammen
tomato	. . . .	die Tomate
tool	. . . .	das Werkzeug
tooth	. . . .	der Zahn
touch	. . . .	berühren
tour	. . . .	die Tour
tower	. . . .	der Turm
town	. . . .	die Stadt
town hall	. . . .	das Rathaus
toy	. . . .	das Spielzeug
traditional	. . . .	traditionell
traffic	. . . .	der Verkehr
transport	. . . .	das Verkehrsmittel
trick	. . . .	der Trick
trip	. . . .	der Ausflug
trousers	. . . .	die Hose
turkey	. . . .	der Truthahn
turn	. . . .	abbiegen
TV	. . . .	der Fernseher

U

uncle	. . . .	der Onkel
under	. . . .	unter
uniform	. . . .	die Uniform
USA	. . . .	die Vereinigten Staaten von Amerika
usage	. . . .	die Nutzung

V

vet	. . . .	der Tierarzt, die Tierärztin
vinegar	. . . .	der Essig
visit	. . . .	besuchen
volleyball	. . . .	der Volleyball, das Spiel Volleyball

W

wait	. . . .	warten
waiter, waitress	. . . . . .	der Kellner, die Kellnerin
want	. . . .	wollen
wash	. . . .	waschen
waste	. . . .	verschwenden
watch	. . . .	beobachten
water	. . . .	das Wasser, gießen
water hose	. . . .	der Wasserschlauch
watering can	. . . .	die Gießkanne
way	. . . .	der Weg
wear	. . . .	tragen
welcome	. . . .	willkommen
what	. . . .	was
when	. . . .	wann
where	. . . .	wo
which	. . . .	welcher, welche, welches
who	. . . .	wer
window	. . . .	das Fenster
with	. . . .	mit
wool	. . . .	die Wolle
work	. . . .	die Arbeit, arbeiten
worried	. . . .	besorgt, beunruhigt
wrapping	. . . .	die Verpackung
write	. . . .	schreiben
wrong	. . . .	falsch

Y

year	. . . .	das Jahr
young	. . . .	jung

Z

zebra	. . . .	das Zebra
zebra crossing	. . . . . .	der Zebrastreifen
zoo	. . . .	der Zoo
zookeeper	. . . .	der Tierpfleger, die Tierpflegerin

A B C D E F G H I J K L M N O P Q R S T U V W X Y Z

Bildquellennachweis:

|Alamy Stock Photo, Abingdon/Oxfordshire: Cavan Images 15.6; Cole, Daniel 43.1; EnVogue_Photo 43.6; Grossman, David 15.1; Levine, Richard 53.4; Palinchak, Mykhailo 28.3; Panther Media GmbH 48.12, 48.13; Sykes, Homer 49.4; Westend61 GmbH 48.11. |Alamy Stock Photo (RMB), Abingdon/Oxfordshire: Art Directors/Rauter, Peter 30.2; Avalon/Bruce Coleman Inc 37.2; Jordan, Peter 36.1; The Photolibrary Wales 49.5; Tripplaar, Kristoffer 41.1. |Assies, Juliane, Berlin: 7.17, 12.1, 12.2, 12.3, 12.4, 12.5, 12.6, 12.7, 12.8, 12.9, 13.1, 13.2, 13.3, 13.4, 13.5, 13.6, 13.7, 13.8, 13.9, 13.10, 13.11, 13.12, 13.13, 13.14, 13.16, 13.19, 14.2, 14.3, 14.4, 14.5, 14.6, 14.7, 14.8, 18.1, 19.1, 19.4, 19.9, 19.10, 19.13, 19.15, 19.17, 24.1, 29.1, 31.3, 31.7, 31.8, 33.19, 34.1, 34.3, 34.5, 34.6, 34.10, 39.20, 58.1, 58.2, 58.8, 58.9, 58.11, 58.12, 58.13, 58.14, 58.15, 59.2, 59.4, 59.8, 59.9, 60.1. |Blanck, Iris, Hamburg: 2.8, 2.9, 2.15, 66.5. |Dölling, Andrea, Berlin: 19.3. |Ehlers, Gisela, Hüttenwohld: 4.12. |fotolia.com, New York: clickit 35.7; Hackemann, Jörg 5.11; Kosmider, Patryk 4.5; lucamedei 4.11; OHRAUGE 5.7; potteret 35.3; rcfotostock 4.6; somartin 4.4; Spencer 5.2. |Getty Images (RF), München: Bobbe, Leland 5.9; Rubberball/Kemp, Mike 5.5. |Hilgert, Gabie, Hamburg: 17.1, 17.2, 17.5, 22.1, 22.2, 22.3, 22.4, 36.7, 36.8, 52.1. |Holzhausen, Elisabeth, Wedel: 60.2, 60.4, 60.5, 60.6, 60.7, 60.8, 60.9, 61.2, 61.3, 61.4, 61.5, 61.6, 61.7, 62.1, 62.2, 62.3, 62.4, 62.5, 62.6, 62.7, 63.1, 63.2, 63.3, 63.4, 63.5, 63.6, 63.7, 63.8. |Humbach, Markus, Osnabrück: 55.10. |Imago, Berlin: imagebroker 31.5; Rudel, Horst 26.1. |iStockphoto.com, Calgary: aabejon 4.8; AleksandaRandjelovic 26.3; Baggett, Anthony 4.10; Davoust, Laurent 5.4; fstop123 53.1; Harding, Ben 28.1; Highwaystarz-Photography 8.8; Locke, Sean 4.7; Moller, Karen 5.6; Pepgooner 23.3; riki76 23.2; Steward, Linda 42.2, 42.3, 42.4; visual7 4.3, 4.9, 5.8, 5.10, 55.9. |Jane Goodall Institute, Vienna: © the Jane Goodall Institute / Courtesy of the Goodall Family 37.1. |juniors@wildlife Bildagentur GmbH, Hamburg: Zoellner, B. 35.5. |mauritius images GmbH, Mittenwald: age/Rupeta, Oleksandr 26.4; Alamy/Atkin, Dan 30.5; Alamy/Levenson, David 30.3, 30.4; Minden Pictures 35.2. |Muth, Matthias, Biederitz: 15.2, 15.3, 15.4, 15.5, 15.7, 28.2, 28.4, 28.5. |Picture-Alliance GmbH, Frankfurt a.M.: dpa 35.6; Photoshot 37.3. |Ruthe, Oda, Braunschweig: 3.4, 6.1, 6.2, 7.3, 7.4, 7.8, 7.9, 7.14, 8.2, 10.1, 11.1, 19.5, 19.11, 20.1, 20.3, 20.4, 20.5, 20.6, 20.7, 20.8, 20.9, 20.10, 20.11, 20.12, 32.2, 33.3, 33.4, 33.6, 33.8, 33.11, 33.13, 33.14, 33.15, 33.16, 33.17, 33.18, 34.2, 34.4, 34.7, 34.8, 34.9, 36.2, 36.3, 36.4, 36.5, 36.6, 38.1, 39.1, 39.2, 39.5, 39.7, 39.8, 39.12, 39.13, 39.14, 39.15, 39.16, 39.17, 44.1, 44.2, 44.3, 45.1, 45.2, 45.3, 45.4, 45.5, 45.6, 46.1, 47.1, 47.2, 47.3, 47.4, 47.5, 47.6, 47.7, 47.8, 47.9, 47.10, 47.11, 47.12, 47.13, 47.14, 47.16, 47.17, 48.1, 48.2, 48.3, 48.4, 48.5, 48.6, 48.7, 48.8, 48.9, 48.10, 49.1, 49.2, 50.1, 50.2, 50.3, 50.4, 50.5, 50.6, 50.7, 50.8, 52.7, 52.17, 55.2, 55.3, 55.4, 55.8, 56.1, 56.2, 56.3, 57.1, 57.2, 57.3, 57.4, 57.5, 58.3, 58.4, 58.5, 58.6, 58.7, 59.3, 59.6, 59.7, 60.3. |Schmidt, Lena, Hannover: 23.6, 23.7, 23.8, 23.9, 23.10, 23.11, 43.4, 43.8. |Schumann, Friederike, Berlin: Titel, Titel, Titel, Titel, 1.1, 1.2, 1.3, 2.1, 2.3, 2.5, 2.10, 2.16, 2.18, 3.1, 3.2, 3.3, 3.5, 3.6, 3.7, 3.8, 3.9, 3.10, 5.1, 7.1, 7.2, 7.5, 7.6, 7.7, 7.10, 7.11, 7.12, 7.13, 7.15, 7.16, 8.1, 8.3, 8.4, 8.5, 8.6, 8.7, 9.1, 13.15, 13.17, 13.18, 19.2, 19.6, 19.7, 19.8, 19.12, 19.14, 19.16, 21.2, 23.1, 25.2, 25.3, 25.4, 25.5, 25.6, 25.7, 25.8, 25.9, 25.10, 25.11, 25.12, 25.13, 25.14, 25.15, 25.16, 25.17, 25.18, 25.19, 27.1, 27.2, 27.3, 27.4, 27.5, 27.6, 27.7, 27.8, 27.9, 27.10, 27.11, 29.2, 29.3, 29.4, 29.5, 29.6, 32.1, 33.1, 33.2, 33.5, 33.7, 33.9, 33.10, 33.12, 35.4, 39.3, 39.4, 39.6, 39.9, 39.10, 39.11, 39.18, 39.19, 40.1, 47.15, 49.3, 51.1, 51.2, 51.3, 51.4, 52.2, 52.3, 52.4, 52.5, 52.6, 52.8, 52.9, 52.10, 52.11, 52.12, 52.13, 52.14, 52.15, 52.16, 54.1, 54.2, 54.3, 54.4, 54.5, 54.6, 55.1, 58.10, 59.1, 59.5, 66.3, 67.1. |Shutterstock.com, New York: de Marmore, Cabeca 16.3; ducu59us 43.5; Kane, Richard Paul 53.3; mangostock 43.7; Monk, Stuart 55.5, 55.7; stuar 16.2; vichie81 55.6. |stock.adobe.com, Dublin: Photographee.eu 31.6; Pixel-Shot 4.1; pololia 5.3; REUTERS/Stapleton, Shannon 53.2; Sanders, Gina 31.4; yamix 4.2; Yoreh 35.1. |Tauber, Andreas, Berlin: 9.2, 14.9, 20.2, 27.12, 27.13, 27.14, 27.15, 34.11, 34.12, 35.8, 40.2, 40.3, 41.2. |vario images, Bonn: Cultura RF 26.2.